A GENTLE WARNING TO THIEVES

This book is the sole personal property of

_____

Any attempt of theft or vandalism of this book shall invoke the **Malay Curse Of the Black Djin** upon the perpetrator.

The curse's effects include, but are not limited to: headaches, blindness, loss of bowel control, diminishing social fortune, boils, toothaches, loss of sexual potency, uncontrolled hair growth, uncontrolled hair loss, lighting strikes from clear skies, tooth loss, unexpected pregnancies, mysterious dogs following your every move, "Super Herpes," childish taunting, horrifying weight gain, sudden loss of family members in thresher accidents, falling anvils, loss of speech, ironic misfortune, ennui, spontaneous human combustion, cancer of the everything, facial tics, violent diarrhea, skin loss, constant circus music, tongue swelling, being turned into a cockroach, being torn apart by flesh-eating birds, itchy palms, developing a thick Scottish accent, and flu-like symptoms.

"Dr. Sketchy's combines three hours of art, booze, hot burlesque performers, circus freaks and hunka-hunka beefcakes. You bring your dip pens and watercolors; Sketchy brings out your artistic talents." —Philladelphia City Paper

"As many varieties of depraved humanity as three hours can hold." —Phoenix New Times

"Frustrated by traditional life-drawing classes?...Dr. Sketchy's Anti-Art School could be the answer....Dr. Sketchy's will cure you of every boring art class you've ever been too....Very Toulouse Lautrec." —Sunday Age (Melbourne)

"Expect to find snarling clowns, glitter, pasties, swords, hula hoops, and more to inspire your next masterpiece." —Village Voice

"At this school it's okay to be hot for teacher, but try to keep your eyes on your own paper." —Fleshbot

"If you're looking for life-drawing classes, forget Pratt. Try Dr. Sketchy's Anti-Art School.... Every other Saturday, burlesque stars...strip down so beer-quaffing Rembrandts can render their forms." —Time Out New York

"Fluid and luscious...Dr. Sketchy's truly brings out the best in its artists." —Brian Wood

"Dr. Sketchy's has gone from New York treasure to international phenomenon in a handful of months: a little piece of imaginary Twenties Paris where anyone who can hold a pencil may sketch beautiful burlesque models . . . only the Manhattan Renaissance Woman that is Molly Crabapple could tell you about it this well." —Warren Ellis, author of Transmetropolitan

"Like the perfect mixed drink, Dr. Sketchy's Official Rainy Day Colouring Book combines one part smooth operation, one party sweetly amorous flirtation, and one part bitterness to make sure it goes down smooth and leaves you swooning afterwards." —Audacia Ray, author of Naked on the Internet

"Dr. Sketchy's is not just a book or a drawing class—its a lifestyle. And not the kind that you not-so-secretly resent other people for having - its a totally accessible DIY lifestyle that you too can possess if you simply follow Molly Crabapple and John Leavitt's instructions." —Audacia Ray, author of Naked on the Internet

"By golly, Miss Molly's book is the perfect combination of cheesecake and mind candy. 100% yummy, brainy decadence." —Lily Burana, author of Strip City and Try

"Speaking as a former artist's model, this hoochie-coo approach to rendering the human form is a lot more rewarding than drawing Spunky from the back of a magazine, especially when cocktails are available on campus." —Ayun Halliday, author of Dirty Sugar Cookies and No Touch Monkey!

DR. SKETCHY'S

OFFICIAL

RAINY DAY

COLOURING

BOOK

BY

MOLLY CRABAPPLE

& JOHN LEAVITT

A Sepulculture Book
Sepulculture DIY Publishing
Brooklyn, New York

A SEPULCULTURE DIY BOOK, DECEMBER 2006

Published in the United States by Sepulculture, Brooklyn NY

Library of Congress Cataloging-in-Publication Data
Dr. Sketchy's Official Rainy Day Colouring Book.
p.   cm.
1. Dr. Sketchy's   2. Art and humor.   I. Title.

Sepulculture ISBN-10: 0-9789534-0-1
Sepulculture ISBN-13: 978-0-9789534-0-9

www.sepulculture.com

Second Edition

Printed in Singapore
10   9   8   7   6   5   4   3   2

Molly would like to acknowledge coffee, Pagan God of Productivity.

Special thanks for Warren Ellis, for his stalwart support,
to Joi and Lilah of the Lucky Cat, Kate Black, Syd Berenstien,
Gary Winter, Ryan Roman, Rachel Kramer Bussel,
and my excellent mother.

Most of all, to Fred Harper, for being a slab of blond beefcake
who draws like the wind.

John Leavitt couldn't have done it with you, yes you.

Thanks to Dr. Simon (AKA Moggie), Syd, Ryan, The Lucky Cat,
Gary Winter, Dottie Lux, Amber Ray, Tangerine Jones,
Ian and Gavin, The White Boom-Boom, Scarlet Sinclair,
Darlinda Just Darlinda, and Lady J.

Special thanks to Nemo, for everything.

www.drsketchy.com

Dr. Sketchy's Official Rainy Day Colouring Book

TABLE OF CONTENTS

INTRODUCTION

$\mathscr{G}$etting naked can change your life. It sure changed mine.

When I was a wee girl in art school, I was very poor. One day, in caffeine-soaked desperation, I sat at a diner with my co-author, John Leavitt, discussing career opportunities. He pointed to two on my chest.

I didn't have the work ethic or the frosted hair for stripping. But I did have gusto and a desire not to starve to death. So I embarked on a journey through New York's nude modeling scene. Over the next two years, I posed for thousands of paintings, photographs, pencil sketches, lithographs and sculptures. I cracked my back in the dank basement of Spring Street Studios. I sat naked on the desks of geriatric illustrators while their home aids looked blithely onwards. I flew to LA and San Francisco and Boston, got picked up in livery cars, spent $400 on corsets, saw the insides of Manhattan's Upper East Side Mansions, and often made over a hundred dollars an hour. I was also often terribly, horribly broke.

Once, a photographer had a heart attack while shooting me.

Stripping was looking better every day.

Two years later, I'm a successful illustrator—though I still don't have that art school degree. For all its skeeziness, I wouldn't have traded my time modeling for any temp career in the world, except for one thing.

Posing for art classes sucks.

I got into the naked girl business thinking art modeling would be the best of it. I pictured Man Ray, Kiki de Montparnasse, a saucy and silk-robed bohemia where morals ran loose and beauty reigned supreme. Oh dear reader, how fast I was disillusioned!

Art modeling pays bupkus, 12-20 bucks an hour for brutal, back-breaking work. What's worse, the class pretends you're not there. In Art's quest for professionalism, the teachers took warm, naked bodies and made them sterile as platonic solids. I'd rather be a pair of tits than an octagon. And I'd rather be a whole person then a pair of tits.

Where was the Montparnasse of my fantasies? And I knew I wasn't alone. Even Dan Clowes admits in Art School Confidential, that he was expecting hot model action. So why should life drawing be so dull?

This idea, combined with posing (drunk and stockinged) at the relatively liberal SOI (Society of Illustrators, an old NYC gentleman's club where illustrators can knock back drinks and pine for the days when they were still important), gave me an idea. I'd start my own class, a terribly bohemian class. The model would get paid bank and treated like a queen; not a faceless form, but a big bursting personality.

I'd been dancing burlesque around the Lower East Side and was awed by the visual culture of the dive bars—the tassels and the sequins and the girl-flesh—I tapped top New York burlesque dancers for the first Dr. Sketchy models.

Add contests, the brothel-red Lucky Cat café, an assistant with a penchant for gin, and Dr. Sketchy's was born. Now, one year later, my baby's all grown up. Nine Dr. Sketchy's sharpen their pencils around the world from Denmark to Australia. Sketchy's spawned sketchbooks and

T.V spots . . . and innumerable drawings. And now out comes this book; chock full of paper dolls and drinking games, with all the illustrative madness of our Lucky Cat sessions.

My eyes tear. Bubbalah, I'm so proud!

So if you're in New York (or Portland or Philly or Detroit or Phoenix or Los Angeles or Norfolk or Randers or Melbourne) walk down to your local Dr. Sketchys and say "Hello." Compliment my baby. And if you live in some godless hole with no Sketchy's remember this: your high school guidance counselor was wrong. You too can find a future with gin and loose women. Nudity can change your life.

Here's your one stop guide to Dr. Sketchy's. Now get drawing!

- Molly Crabapple
  Williamsburg

A SKETCHY SCRAMBLE

Unscramble the following letters to solve the riddle below. Or else!

How Dr. Sketchy lives:

nsi ni

The best kind of exposure:

dwel

What happens right before vomit:

outgrt

The bane of all Art Monkeys:

perap⁻tucs

Goes great with coffee:

bamcusa

What keeps us decent:

tspeisa

What are the loosest things at an Anti⁻Art School?

— — — — — —

4

CAN YOU DRAW "MADDY"?

Can't get to an Anti-Art School? Don't worry! The ALL NEW Dr. Sketchy's Anti-Art School Correspondence course allows even the most paranoid hermit to enjoy the wonders of an Anti-Art School education.

SEND NO MONEY Simply draw the model on this page and send it by electronic mail to Dr. Sketchy's Correspondence Center. Once there, teams of highly trained Art Monkeys will evaluate your drawing and may select you to join our Elite Mail-Order Sketch Academy. You'll be given full course materials as well as your own tassels and feathered boas to fully re-create the Dr. Sketchy's experience in the comfort of your own home, detention facility, or isolated mountain cabin.

Don't delay! If you can draw Maddy The Model, you may be on your way to fame and fortune!

DR. SKETCHY'S ANTI-ART CORRESPONENCE SCHOOL
1113 LOST MAIDENHEAD LANE
CAPITAL CITY, KHAZAR
I C K 9 - 0 0 2 3

THE IDEAL CHOICE FOR ARTISTS *ON THE GO!*

THE HISTORY OF DR. SKETCHY'S

by J. Leavitt, noted scholar

The first known reference to Dr. Sketchy comes from Imperial Rome. In 31 B.C.E., an informal academy for fresco painters was founded in the crowded Subura district. It attracted many respectable artists and models and once featured Livia herself (in disguise, of course). Alas, like so much of Rome, by 64 A.D. it had become a den of hard drink, loose women, and off-key poets. Eventually the entire enterprise was run out of Rome when the artists couldn't prove that they had nothing to do with that fire.

A thousand years later, Roman retro was all the rage. Verme Bozetto re-founded Dr. Sketchy's in 1431 in Florence but quickly abandoned it in 1432 after concerns about artistic theft and unflattering caricatures of the Medicis. Bozetto moved Dr. Sketchy's to Venice. However, an increase in canal deaths of vino-soaked art students forced Verme to move again. He resurfaced in Bruges in 1434, only to be beaten to death by ruffians a year later after making several loud, despairing remarks about Flemish cuisine in public.

Here the records grow spotty. An Ottoman decree in 1545 banned "lewd heathen drawings in coffeeshops." A small reference to an "Unwholesome Sketche Clubbe" by Samuel Pepys in 1667. In 1780, there is mention of a shadowy "Dr. Croquis Society" founded by Cagliostro in France. Supposedly, "Dr. Croquis" had great occult powers and sway over important figures. A royal investigation was created to snuff out "Croquis" but later dropped when it was discovered that the society was just an excuse to get aristocratic women naked so Cagliostro could steal their jewels.

The modern history of Dr. Sketchy's Anti-Art School begins in 1896, with an advertisement in the Yellow Book promising "A Most Delightful and Bizarre Sketch Session for Gentlemen of a Sensitive, Aesthetic nature." Held in the "Cafe du Chat Chanceux" in Paris, Dr. Sketchy's was hosted by the mysterious "Marquis de Escroquerie" and featured lively Can-Can dancing, absinthe drinking contests, and more than one hissy slap fight.

World War One forced the aged Marquis to Berlin where (now known as Count Von Skizze) he reopened the Anti-Art School at the Kit Kat Cafe in 1924. Sadly, two years later, a group of addled Surrealists, driven mad by model Anita Berber, destroyed the Kit Kat in a mass of ink bombs and fish throwing. Andre Breton considered restarting it, but was put off by the weight of modeling lamps. Count Von Skizze died in 1927, leaving behind his estate to his son, Jacob, who promptly spent it all on booze and women, dying in a heated poker game three years later.

Anita Berber's Svengali, The Baron von Droste, took up Dr. Sketchy's torch and brought it to New York, where it served as an ongoing cubist art project at Mabel Dodge's salon. Sadly, Dr. Sketchy's met an unfortunate end (along with the rest of Mabel Dodge's salon) after an ill-fated peyote-and-dressup party.

In 2004 artist's model and illustrator, Molly Crabapple, discovered the "lost" Dr. Sketchy documents inside a giraffe-upholstered chair at the Duc de Ventre's Central Park West studio. The bizarre drawings, complete with a rambling account of the history of Dr. Sketchy's, inspired Ms. Crabapple. She begged the Duc de Ventre to let her have them in lieu of payment for her modeling services. He agreed and she reopened Dr. Sketchy's Anti-Art School in 2005, where it continues, in a much less psychedelic form, to this day in Brooklyn.

A Super-Fun Dr. Sketchy's Colouring Book Page!
Dr. Sketchy himself!

10

Above: Miss Allison at Dr. Sketchy's NYC, photographed by Dr. Simon
Below: A horde of Art Monkeys, photographed by Ryan Roman

Art Monkey and Photo Monkey Ryan Roman at the Lucky Cat

AN AMAZING WORD FIND!

Can you find all these words in this tangled mess of random letters? I know you can.

Gin Tassels Espresso Glitter Inkwell Nude
Model Paint Bar Bohemian Brush Vodka Boa

```
H A W T H A W T A L L N U E S T O
E E R T A S S E L S V J U Y L O B N A
A P E G T P A B E U Y A I L O S J D Q
G F A B R Y U O V O D K A Y T S X O
I H E I L E A V I T Z N U M Q A A B
N G U N E O P L K U E S P R E S S O
I I U Z W T B A D D D B R S S E L A A
M O L S T A A R T S A E O I N O W H S
G L I T T E R A S S P U Y N N B R U S H
Z H N A L L T H E T I M E Z H O R U M S
A S H K A L L G I R L S J W A H Q W E A
I U Y A W D A N S E C O N T E M I A N
J A C K O F C I R C L E J E R M O W
M A S T E R B A T E S T R H I A K O L
T O R S O B R E A S T I S C L I C O O
N A K E D L S U C K N N D O N N U D E
```

The Dr. Sketchy's Anti-Art Correspondence School Official Home Burlesque Kit

Can't find lively dancing girls in your one-horse town? Not a problem! Simply cut out and color these Official Anti-Art Correspondence School pasties and soon you'll be strutting and stripping to the delight and horror of young and old alike!

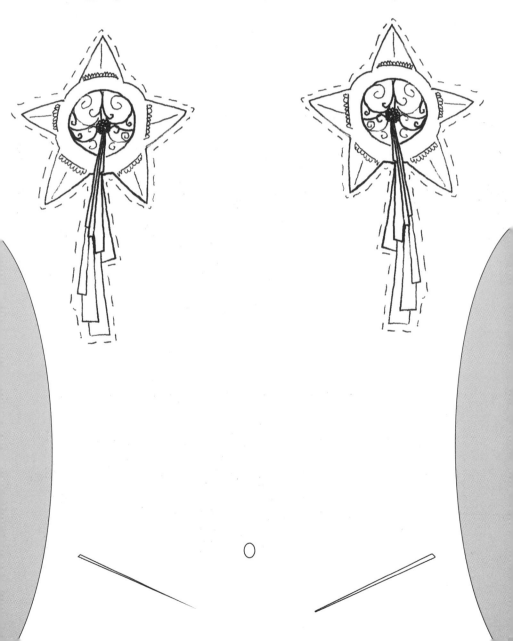

The History of Dr. Sketchy's That's Not a Complete Lie

By Molly Crabapple

The idea for Dr. Sketchy's spent a long time fermenting. I'd long fantasized about running a life drawing class just the way I wanted. After many hours spent bullshitting in my atelier (i.e. a unfurnished tenement apartment in Brooklyn), Leavitt and I decided to hold "Muse and Monster" sketch sessions in my hospital-green living room. We only got as far as the flyer design, but still forced our well-meaning friends to strip for us as we got progressively wasted on alco-pops.

Those were the days.

However, it wasn't sitting around drinking that got me thinking about how to improve life drawing classes. Harsh experience on the model stand did that. Modeling for art classes is the ugly but respectable sister of the time I spent jumping naked on beds and covering myself in cherry sauce for the cameras of highly-suspect photographers. Sure, you don't have to worry about getting raped posing for a life drawing class, but you don't get $125 an hour either. Posing for artists filled the gaps in my "internet modeling" schedule.

I still had dreams of being an artist, dreams that did not match my current reality. Remember the aforementioned unfurnished room? Thankfully, my life had improved since I started art school. At least I was no longer sharing a studio with two bossy Korean Baptists and their non-English speaking mom. I had a window, if not chairs. But I still wasn't the jetsetting proto-Warhol that Hollywood assured me I'd be. I spent seven hours a day going to the Fashion Institute of Technology for illustration, and seven more actually trying to get work. I had no ins, no leads, a dwindling bank account, and an all Snickers diet.

What I lacked in smart business connections I made up for in unabashed chutzpa. I drew a lot at cafes to avoid going back to my bleak 5th floor walk-up. My first sold painting was to the burly proprietor of Espresso Thyself, a coffee shop near FIT that also functioned as my office, living room, spa, and primary source of day old muffins. He hung it proudly behind the counter, giving me the idea to hang shows in bars and cafés. I'd be a bohemian star! Underground bar artist!

It didn't work out that way.

My first show at Rain Lounge was the sort of failure that crushes dreams into a fine paste. The bartender tore down my posters. The help broke my frames. The owner didn't recognize me. The paintings were in complete darkness. No one showed up.

I then tried to get illustration work. The head of The New York Times Book Review glanced at my portfolio and told me he only hired "intelligent artists." I harassed anyone and everyone with my pack of 30-dollar business cards, which lead to a few "lunch meetings" with morbidly obese comics geeks who stared down my dress. Even the anarchist bookstore rejected my work. Mine was a life of making oneself the constant focus of attention, the bright bulb that would never shut off. I must have been an obnoxious little shit.

If nothing else, tireless self-promotion tought me the hard lesson that success in a creative field does not hinge on being smarter or more talented than anyone else. Rather, it depends on being an endless sponge to soak up whole universes of humiliation and defeat. Self-promotion is constantly throwing a birthday where no one shows up. It requires the delusion that you can convince people to pay you for doing what you want to do.

One of those psychotic flights of fancy did bear fruit however. I had been going to burlesque shows around town, entranced by a glittering world of costumes, honky-tonk piano, and bouncing flesh. Sure it was stripping, but it was amazing, witty, hilarious stripping with feather boas and tassels. One troupe, IXON Burlesque, ran an arch-traditional show, complete with a live band. I got up the courage to ask the director if I could maybe perhaps design a poster for them? I got the job and the opportunity to hang out backstage with beautiful women and finally live out a Toulouse-Lautrec fantasy. My confidence grew and as girls dropped out, I eventually ended up in the show. I started booking myself into small burlesque shows, making friends with organizers and girls, and was amazed they let little uncoordinated me dance in front of paying customers.

Meanwhile, my boyfriend of four years ditched me to spend more time alone in his room with The Cure. I reacted with fervent lesbianism. After dispatching a flaky artists' model and a Puerto-Ricana army private, I met Jen Dziura. Jen Dziura was an ivy-league educated lingerie model with an ass that got her jobs as a body double and the face of Madame X. She came up to New York after the dot-com implosion ate her web design company. With her intelligence, sarcasm and ruthless ambition, Jen became my bestest friend. But, friend or no, I couldn't help envying her success as a comedian/producer. Particularly when one of her shows, the Williamsburg Spelling Bee, landed her razor cheekbones on the cover of The New York Times.

I was still breaking my back as a model.

Damn her.

Goaded by jealousy, that fermenting idea in the back of my mind began to take shape. Slowly it dawned on me that I could cobble together the jagged fragments of my life into one glittering pastiche.

I could do an event.

From burlesque shows, I got costuming, staging and acquaintance with rosters of girls named Trixie.

From showing art in bars I learned how to promote events in the face of mass indifference.

From Jen and her spelling bee, I learned the importance of audience participation.

From art modeling I learned what not to do.

I already had a friendly in with a venue: the Lucky Cat.

Originally, my co-creator A.V. Phibes would co-host with me. She's since left to turn her attention to matters that actually make money. A.V. designed our first flyers and cobbled together a website. I emailed Dottie Lux, a burlesque clown, got a date, and the first Dr. Sketchy's burst forth, fully clothed, from Zeus' brow.

Of course, there was more to it than that.

I got to meet the owners of the Lucky Cat when producing a benefit for my friend Lola Ramona, who lost all her stuff in an unfortunate sprinkler accident. It was a smash, of course, but I was working for charity then. Now I was entering into the thankless pit-fight that constitutes "fun" in New York.

The first Dr. Sketchy's in the frigid December of 2005, was attended by anyone we could guilt into coming (yes, including my mom). I made a cool 30 bucks, blown on celebratory martinis afterwards. But I had gained something else, the iron confidence that comes from producing something that isn't a flop.

After that, I applied the black magic of marketing towards making Dr. Sketchy's a success. I'm the sort of girl who haunts the business section at book stores, taking frantic notes on PR for Dummies. I eat business books, and occasionally fancy myself a cash-obsessed yuppie, until I actually meet one. In Williamsburg, Adam Smith hangs with

Hitler. Yet there's no reason your wacky bohemian hobbies shouldn't pay off. By the second Dr. Sketchy's, summoning capitalist Cthulhu paid off. Dr. Sketchy's was a hit.*

For the second Dr. Sketchy's, Amber Ray came in glistening with 5,000 rhinestones and a white wig that made her look like topless Madame de Pompadour. And the people! We packed fifty patrons into the back room of the Lucky Cat, violating several fire regulations, and causing at least three incidents of unintentional sexual harassment. As Phibes and I divvied up the stacks of twenties, we felt finally that sensation that had been missing since grade school.

They liked us! They really, really liked us!

One of my primary weapons in getting asses into seats was this "Internet." First, Phibes created a website and coerced her intern to design posters. In order to create buzz I needed tons of sexy, sexy photographs. And not the typical flash snapshot; mood lighting. So I called on one of the best photographers from my bad old modeling days, Gary Winter. Gary was a documentary photographer who haunted the Slipper Room shooting the dancers. He was all too ready for a chance to photograph half-nude burlesque girls in an unusual setting.

My co-author Leavitt took control of the blog, recapping the week's events with acerbic wit and many photos. Constant "informing" via e-mail finally got me the Time Out and Daily Candy listings I craved. Thus the marketing juggernaut was in place.

It wasn't all peaches and sunshine. Once, the MTA shut down all train service to Williamsburg during a sketch session. We compensated by pasting posters of sword-wielding nymphettes all over the neighborhood. It packed the house. Our worst fears came true however, when in front of fifty people and a television crew, our world-famous model didn't show up. Undaunted, I raced home, dug out my smuttiest, spangliest bikini, and

*For a hint of these marketing ideas, see the "How to" section of this book

showed I still had those artist model chops after all.

With our friendly and gorgeous models, our heavy drinking, and our fabulous contests, we soon got what amounted to a (very) small cult following. Our patrons became "Art Monkeys," a term borrowed from the Madagascar Institute after an ill-advised night spent designing steel weasels at their Gowanas headquarters. Some of the Art Monkeys graduated to Helper Monkey status, by virtue of showing up all the time to ask if they could help. Syd Berstein was a devotee of Jen Dzuira, who I recruited into my dark service. Steve Walker provided web help and a Mohawk that had all the ladies drooling. Ryan Roman soon became our de-facto photographer, partly due to talent, and partly because his photos make me look hot.

I took to spamming the LiveJournal Illustrator's group. This drummed up a lot of enthusiasm and a lot of people who complained, "This sounds so cool! Why can't we have one in Omsk?" Taking a page from Stitch-n-Bitch and my dreams of running a cult, I wrote a "How to Start Your Own Dr. Sketchy's" article and posted it on the site. The first Dr. Sketchy's satellite was founded by underground artist Jason Levesque (Aka "Stuntkid") in Norfolk, Virginia, a town once described by Tangerine Jones as "nothing but slurpees, 7-Elevens, and Jesus." Later, Mike Schwartz took it international with a Dr. Sketchy's in Randers, Denmark. For more on those wacky Dr. Sketchy scions, read Chapter Six.

For what started out as another half-baked idea I never expected to finish, Dr. Sketchy's has ended up taking over my life. I owe it all too amazing friends, who where so supportive, so enthusiastic, and so willing to work for free; also to the same hubris and disregard for other people's time that I learned in the naked girl business. So thank you, all you little Art Monkeys sketching away in the dark.

I'm ready for my close-up Mr. DeMille.

A Super-Fun Dr. Sketchy's Colouring Book Page!
Dottie Lux: The very first Dr. Sketchy's model!

22

Dottie Lux,
photographed by
Gary Winter

Dottie Lux with cake and costume, photographed by Ryan Roman

OH NO!

Dr. Sketchy has lost his precious booze again! Can you help him find all the missing bottles of moonshine in this picture of Lolita Haze, nymphet seductress of Dr. Sketchy's Phoenix?

Answer: 14 Bottles, you lush.

25

PAPER DOLLS

You'll have hours of fun with these darling paper dolls! Simply cut out the bodies and costumes and indulge your hidden desires as you mix and match their fabulous accessories!

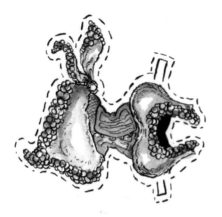

Amber Ray, muse, photographed by Gary Winter

Amber Ray, photographed by Gary Winter

A History of Depraved Life Drawing

*N*udity can change the world. The following people grinned and bared it, leaving the world just a bit more interesting.

★ Galatea - Ancient Greece

Created by master sculptor Pygmalion, Galatea was the most beautiful ivory figure ever made. Naturally, he had to fuck it. Sadly, warms-with-you-vibrating-cyber-skin was a few thousand years off. So Aphrodite blessed the statue with life; saving Pygmalion many an aching hand and creating a reputation for model sluttiness that persists to this day.

★ Phryne - Circa 4th Century Thebes

Another hot-to-trot Greek, Phryne was Greece's most celebrated courtesan, posing for many a marble Venus. When the jealous wives of Athens came to put her on trial for mocking the Eleusian mysteries, she stripped bare and declared "Could anything this beautiful be capable of evil?" She got off.

★ Michelangelo - Florence, Italy 1475-1564

Painter, sculptor, Renaissance man, you know the guy. Check out his women from time to time. Breasts have shriveled to the size of knobby cherries and migrated to the shoulders. Women with thighs that could crush a man's head. Check out Night's lantern jaw. Not surprisingly, this did not create a new standard of female beauty. Though his "friend" Tomosso made a fetching Cleopatra.

34

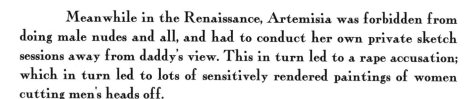

★ Artemisia Gentileschi - Italy 1593-1653

Meanwhile in the Renaissance, Artemisia was forbidden from doing male nudes and all, and had to conduct her own private sketch sessions away from daddy's view. This in turn led to a rape accusation; which in turn led to lots of sensitively rendered paintings of women cutting men's heads off.

★ Titian - Venus of Urbino 1538

With her luscious skin, flowing red hair, and come hither eyes it's no surprise this was made for a man's bedroom. Venus' frank eroticism and lack of classic allegory stunned early viewers. Remember, as Molly does, it's not porn if it's in a gold frame.

★ Ingres v. Delacroix - France 1780-1860

Up until Ingres, most models had been male. Ingres made female models respectable for the academy by making them respectfully chaste. He was still condemned as a rebel by classicists. His hot blooded competitor Delacroix practiced his drawing in Moroccan brothels, leading to less modest Odalisques and more Deaths of Sardanapalus.

★ John Ruskin - England 1840s

Academy painters in England learned to draw from plaster casts of statues. John Ruskin, so used to the chaste whiteness of the casts, was struck permanently impotent when his bride revealed she had hair down there.

★ Model's Market - Paris 1860s-1900

In Montmartre, Paris models hung out around a fountain waiting to be picked up by passing artists. Whole families would stake out, from Granddad (Moses) to the baby (Jesus). Nice work if you can get it.

Manet - Olympia 1863

Manet's blunt courtesan shocked and appalled 19th century France, causing the painting to be banned from the Paris Salon of 1863. His crime? Placing a lady of "leisure" in the same pose as the now respectable Venus of Urbino. Funny how quickly people forget. As Sister Wendy points out, the gentlemen of the Salon would be all to familiar with Olympia's steely, professional gaze. The model, Victorine Meauret, later became a hot-shot painter in her own right before succumbing to the bottle.

John Singer Sargent & Madame X - Paris 1884

Sargent's scandalous painting of society lady Virginie Amelie Avegno Gautreau, was one shoulder strap away from ignominy. Her family had her name taken off the painting and the shoulder strap painted back on.

Bal des Quartz Arts - Paris 1890

A yearly ball for art students started in the 1890s. The first one was marred by models wearing only body paint, and grasping art students given barrels of free booze. The models ended up fleeing the party for their own safety.

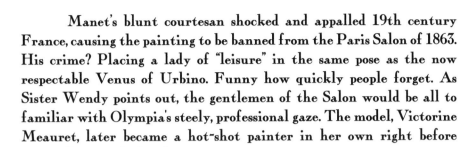

George du Maurier - Trilby 1894

A novel in which the chaste, mannish artist's model Trilby has a platonic affair with the wispy art student who draws her. The sinister Jew (with an Italian name) Svengali uses his magical Jew powers to turn her into an opera singer and lead her into a life of degradation. Considered to be the ur-text for later depictions of bohemia. Also notable for the caricature of Whistler as the "idle apprentice" which led to one of Whistler's many, many lawsuits.

Kiki de Montparnasse – France 1901-1953

Though she ended as a drug addict on the skids, Kiki was perhaps the most beloved artist's model of the age. Born Alice Prinn in the countryside, she bobbed her hair, donned black eyeliner and seduced Man Ray. At 28 she was declared Queen of Montparnasse for her outspoken, wild ways. Her back graces tacky Parisian postcards to this day.

 ### Anita Berber – Berlin 1920s

Weimar Berlin brought scantily-clad women on stage for "Beauty Evenings" where boozy artists would draw them and get blowjobs under the table. Anita Berber, starting as a dancer, posed for a series of etchings that even in that decadent age got confiscated by the police.

 ### Picasso – 1881-1973

Picasso maintained he slept with every one of his female models. Except Gertuide Stien.

 ### Tom of Finland – 1920-1991

Assless chaps ahoy! A pioneer in male erotic nudes, Tom of Finland's distorted, leather fever drawings competed with the more respectable Paul Cadmus. At the Tom Of Finland Art Fair, you can still draw bulging muscle men to this day.

 ### Ayn Rand – The Fountainhead 1943

Ayn Rand took an unfortunate stab at describing the inner life of art modeling in The Fountainhead. Capitalist cutie Dominique Francon poses for a statue of Victory Of the Human Spirit, maintaining perfect ecstasy the entire time. No one is that Objectivist.

Salvador Dali - 1960s

Everyone knows about the melting clocks and watches, but did you know that in the 1960s, Dali trolled the beaches of Spain, picking up hippie kids and making them model on transparent cushions while masturbating wildly behind his canvas. He returned them to their friends days later, shaken to their cores.

Pratt Drawathon - 1990s-Present

A New York City institution and father of Dr. Sketchy's. The Pratt Drawathon brings together hundreds of art students, dozens of models, and unlimited caffeine for a twelve hour all-night art orgy. There's even drumming.

Dr. Sketchy's Anti-Art School - 2005-Present

Of course.

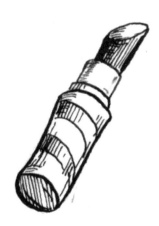

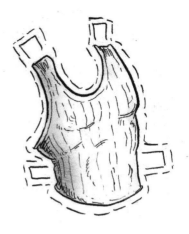

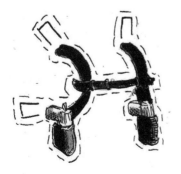

The White Boom Boom,
now sadly clothed, with
adoring Art Monkeys,
photographed by Jo
Boobs, creator of the
burlesque resource site
www.gstringsforever.com

The White Boom Boom, rockabilly hunk, strutting his stuff
at Dr. Sketchy's NYC, photographed by Ryan Roman.

A Super-Fun Dr. Sketchy's Colouring Book Page!
John Leavitt: Co-Author Of this Book and Illustrator

SKETCH WORLD

The satellite Dr. Sketchy's began with a "How To Start Your Own Dr. Sketchy's" essay on the website. These people took up the call and through gumption, grit, and glitter, transformed their towns into hot beds of booze, girls, and paint.

Interviews by Molly Crabapple, girl reporter.

DR. SKETCHY'S RANDERS

Mike Schwartz

Artist, owner of Atalier Mimo and harsh
principal of Dr. Sketchy's Denmark

Tell me a bit about the art scene in Randers? Is it crazy?
Decadent? Nonexistant? What part do you think Dr. Sketchy's plays in
it?

Randers is a small socialist town in the redneck part of Denmark.
The Randers art scene is very "alive" in the sense that every housewife
and family therapist has tried to "find themselves" via a local drawing
class. Everyone in Denmark seems to be making art—but only a few can
really "paint."

Besides the amateurs we have a small crowd of real professionals
here—some of them have been making a living on "art" for more than 20
years. Because of the competition most of us "adapt" to circumstances
match our paintings with the client's sofa. . . .

Dr. Sketchy's Randers, hosted by a professional penniless artist,
will cross borders and build bridges between those housewives . . . and us.

What made you interested in sucking it up and producing your
own Dr. Sketchy's?

I'm your number one stalker, Molly. I'd probably even wear your
bra if you'd let me. Besides that Dr. Sketchy's is just a good concept. The
idea is new here—everyone I've been talking to here loves it and it's good
way of promoting my atelier. Also audience appreciated that because it's
a better use of a Sunday afternoon than playing video games.

What do you do in real life?

After moving to Denmark with only 2 suitcases (because I felt like it) and then realizing that this wasn't a terribly smart move for a broke ex-army guy to do, I ran into a local painter. After two bottles of wine, I made very dirty jokes about the "proportions" of the figures in his paintings. He forced me to paint to prove I could do better. Now four years later I still paint ... for a living.

Has it been easy to get models?

According to local sayings Randers is known for three things: the salmon in the river of Gudenaa, the production of gloves, and the beautiful girls. Well—the salmon are dead because of the pollution, the manufacture of gloves stopped after the company ran bankrupt, and the first Dr. Sketchy's Randers model is Agata from Poland.

Was it easy or difficult to talk a venue into letting you put on debauched life drawing?

It was in fact very easy. Quake, the only cocktail bar in town, gave the green light at the very first approach. They were a bit disappointed when they got my note that the girl will not be "all naked." After she agreed to "at least" go topless they were really happy. Same for our major sponsor Laesehesten (the best, biggest, DVD, PS2-game, ect. shop in town). They immediately said yes.

DR. SKETCHY'S MELBOURNE

http://empe.customer.netspace.net.au/

A Super-Fun Dr. Sketchy's Colouring Book Page!
Doloras Daiquiri: Model for Dr. Sketchy's Melbourne

Melanie Knight

Talented headmistress of Dr. Sketchy's
Melbourne

I have self diagnosed allergy to keeping still. I'm always plotting, scheming and drafting new ideas and plans to take on. I've been drawing anddaydreaming as long as I can remember. I still have the illustrations of Greek Gods I did back as a kid. I spend my time illustrating my favourite early 20TH century French crime novels, on tattoo designs or painting, decorating and fancifying my old furniture. I once had a solo show "Exoteric Melanie - The conspiracy of the Iced Vovo." It had a lot of vaginas and reflected my self-concocted conspiracy about Arnott's desire for yonic expression via the aesthetics of the yummy Iced VoVo biscuit. People were frightened by the paintings but quite enjoyed the Iced VoVos! I also love making posters and album covers and other designs for people!

Tell me a bit about the art scene in Melbourne? Is it crazy? Decadent? Nonexistant? And what part do you think Dr. Sketchy's plays in it?

Melbourne is lucky enough to be overrun with artists of all descriptions, from crazy street art exploding out of all of Melbourne's little alleys and laneways, to sculpture parks, arts and crafts markets every weekend, artist run initiatives and gallery spaces and a constant calendar of festivals! Dr Sketchy's slots right in somewhere between the woman that paints portraits on fingernails and the fetish inspired midget dancing queen!

What made you interested in sucking it up and producing your own Dr. Sketchy's?

A serendipitous blend of having the desire to find a more inspiring reason to get out to life drawing classes and being a long time admirer of Molly's illustrations led me to plucking up the nerve to scout out how to set up Dr Sketchy's in Melbourne and let Molly know how much it would be loved!

What do you do in real life? Are you a professional artist, or just a devotee of drawing scantily clad girls?

Professional is not the word I like to attribute to myself—it's far too serious for me! Apart from organizing and hosting Dr Sketchy's in Melbourne I work full time for a great Orchestra here in Melbourne. The rest of my time is spent painting and decorating my old furniture, illustrating my very favorite early 20th century crime novels, collecting 1st edition books, and attempting to get myself a tattoo apprenticeship. The rest of my time is spent day-dreaming about living inside of a giant, bejeweled elephant just like Satine in Moulin Rouge!

Has it been hard or easy to get models?

There is a fantastic amount of beautiful burlesque babes, circus performers, cabaret acts, belly dancers and fetish enthusiasts to hopefully have a long list of Dr Sketchy's models. So far, every model that has been approached has been as equally beautiful and charming posing as they usually are performing on stage. What performer wouldn't want to be drawn by a room full of people?

Have you encountered any local resistance?

I'd love a bit of local resistance! None as yet, I'm more worried about local indifference. Only thing is all the local bands covering the Dr. Sketchy posters with their own in the laneways, which annoys the bejeebers outta me! All's fair in love and art I suppose.

Was it easy or difficult to talk a venue into letting you put on some debauched life drawing?

The Butterfly Club is a magical little cabaret club full of kitsch and wonderful delights and fairy lights! It is my dream venue and the perfect match for Dr Sketchy's Melbourne. I think my knack for over preparing and their openness made it quite an easy decision to make The Butterfly Club Dr Sketchy's home in Melbourne.

How's the session going? Do you have any crazy stories? Lying absolutely encouraged.

It's been an absolute smash thus far! We've had sketchers travel over an hour just to come along to the session and I've even had enquiries from interstate people popping Dr Sketchy's into their holiday calendar when visiting Melbourne! I have a booking coming up next session for an elderly lady just recently out of hospital and completely wrapped at the thought of coming out at night to draw again and have some fun!

DR. SKETCHY'S NORFOLK

http://stuntkid.com/drsketchys/

A Super-Fun Dr. Sketchy's Colouring Book Page!
Audra Gwarskitty: International Fetish Diva and Model for Dr. Sketchy's Norfolk

Jason Levesque, aka Stuntkid

Hotshot illustrator, digital colouring god, and founder of Dr. Sketchy's Norfolk, our very first branch

Tell me a bit about the art scene in Norfolk. Is it crazy? Decadent? Nonexistant? And what part do you think Dr. Sketchy's plays in it?

Norfolk has been a pretty dead. It's a Navy town with many transient families. Lately though I've seen several forces trying to inspire a local art scene. We've recently seen "First Fridays" started in the Ghent area of Norfolk. A new local online Forum (prettytasty.org) has been launched and we finally have our very own chapter of the AIGA, although I never go. Dr. Sketchy's is definitely playing an important part in our growing art community.

What made you interested in sucking it up and producing your own Dr. Sketchy's?

I'd have to say that your photos from Dr. Sketchy's had me jealous. After some time started a local group in my area. If I wasn't able to get myself to her Sketchy's sessions I'd do what I could to bring them to me.

What do you do in real life? Are you a professional artist, or just a devotee of drawing scantilly clad girls?

By day, my mild mannered alter ego spends time as an Art Director for an internet based company. By night, I slip into my cape and tights and perform the duties of a freelance illustrator.

Has it been hard or easy to get models?

Finding models has not been a problem at all. The girls have all been excited to take part. Our only problem has been finding people that won't back out. It's a good idea to have a backup model close by.

Have you encountered any local resistance?

Nothing so far *knocks on wood*.

Was it easy or difficult to talk a venue into letting you put on some debauched life drawing?

We were lucky, when we first asked around we got several positive responses. It came down to choosing the best location.

How's the session going? Do you have any crazy stories?

Our turnout is growing. The summer is slow but these things can take time to build. We have a group of regulars which is good and the modelsalways have a great time. We are looking forward to the fall when we can approach the college professors about promoting our group.

Tell me a bit about the art scene in your city? Is it crazy? Decadent?

DR. SKETCHY'S PHOENIX

http://www.antiartschool.com/blog/index.php

Dr. Sketchy's Official Rainy Day Colouring Book

A Super-Fun Dr. Sketchy's Colouring Book Page!

Diabolica Robotica: Model for Dr. Sketchy's Phoenix

Rachel Bess

Classical surrealist painter and
co-organizer of Dr. Sketchy's Phoenix

Tell me a bit about the art scene in your city?
Is it crazy? Decadent? Nonexistent? What
part do you think Dr. Sketchy's plays in it?

Contrary to popular belief, the art scene in Phoenix has little to
no Cowboys and Indians. High brow and low brow are both flourishing
quite well here, and as it turns out both clubs are interested in sexy and/or
bizarre naked folks. Dr Sketchy's has brought even more artists and
aspiring artists out of the woodwork . . . it's amazing what a few pierced
nipples can do!

What made you interested in sucking it up and producing your
own Dr. Sketchy's?

Let's see, what about drawing lovely models in latex, lace, roller-
skates and glittery pasties was appealing to me? Aside from my painting,
my day job is to teach "standard" life drawing at a charter arts school out
here. And after many years of the usual life drawing models, it feels as
though you're missing something—a spaced-out woman slouching on a
fold-up chair just doesn't do it for you anymore. Along comes Dr. Sketchy's
to fill that void!

What do you do in real life? Are you a professional artist, or just
a devotee of drawing scantily clad girls?

In real life I'm a painter, and I teach life drawing. Although
perhaps I could just change my job title to encompass both and be a
professional devotee of rendering scantily-clad girls! When I was about 13,
and really starting to get into drawing, I tried to convince my father that
in order to become a better artist, I needed to draw from naked people, and

I gave him some line about the Old Masters. Of course the best resource I could think of for this was porno mags, so I tried and tried to convince him to by me some Club Internationals or Playboys or whatever. I almost had him too, then my mom found out about my plan to draw sexy ladies and she crushed it like a bug!

Has it been hard or easy to get models?

So far it's been quite easy. There's a plethora of talent out there in the underground (and above ground too) and those people are just as eager to model and show off their talents (and make some cash) as we are to draw them.

Have you encountered any local resistance?

Not yet, so far the only resistance we've had was too many people trying to get through the door at one time.

Was it easy or difficult to talk a venue into letting you put on some debauched life drawing?

Our venue, The Trunk Space, was extremely happy to receive us. It's a great space and wonderfully situated next door to a Tiki dive bar that sells $1 PBR's the night of our event. Which is good, because AZ liquor laws prohibit us from having booze at our event (although there are Choco Tacos, coffee and a wide variety of bizarre sodas).

How's the session going? Do you have any crazy stories?

So far it's been awesome, the Phoenix sessions are run a bit like three hour strip teases. Our models show up with lots of layers of exciting apparel and we have a stylist, Melinda Crick, that does amazing things with the model's hair and make-up on site. The model begins posing in full gear and then removes more and more clothing with each pose until they're stripped down to pasties and a corset or sometimes to just their nail polish and tattoos.

DR. SKETCHY'S DETROIT

http://www.drsketchydetroit.blogspot.com

Sparkly Devil of Dr. Sketchy's Detroit,
where winning drawings are signed
with a kiss.

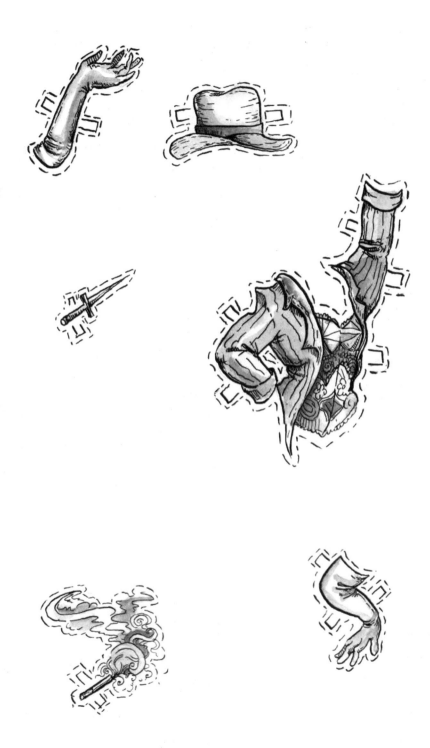

Sean Bieri
Founder of Dr. Sketchy's Detroit

Tell me a bit about the art scene in Detroit. Is it crazy? Decadent? Nonexistent? And what part do you think Dr. Sketchy's plays in it?

To tell the truth, I'm not too much in touch with the art scene in Detroit as such. I get the impression it's like most things in Detroit: scrappy, gritty, fringe-y, living by the seat of its pants, wide open to anyonewho decides they want to make their mark.

The town I live in, Hamtramck, is a small, independent city within Detroit's borders with cheap housing, a large immigrant population from all over the world and a good-sized population of artists. Lately, the art scene's been hurting here in Hamtown: we lost our two main hangouts (the Urban Break coffee shop closed, and then the Salvador Deli burned down), the local pop-art gallery essentially closed, and the artists who moved here in the '90s were all feeling a little scattered, I think. Several local artists are now trying to band together and start a collective called Hatch, that'll keep us in contact with each other and vibrant and relevant in the community.

The Dr. Sketchy project here is the first official event sponsored by the Hatch group.

What made you interested in sucking it up and producing your own Dr. Sketchy's?

What's not to like? I read about it in the 'zine "Croq" (which I by chance picked up at Wholly Craft! in Columbus). Dr. Sketchy sounded like it had all the elements us Detroiters like in our art: sex, booze and rock 'n' roll, but also a communal, grassroots, fuck-the-man sort of aesthetic... perfect! And too many of the artists I know, me included, had gotten away from drawing from life since college, so this was a fun way to get us to do something that's good for us. Like Flintstones vitamins.

What do you do in real life? Are you a professional artist, or just a devotee of drawing scantily clad girls?

I'm the design director for the local alt-weekly, Metro Times, as well as a small-press mini-comics cartoonist and printmaker (with my trusty Print Gocco!)

Has it been hard or easy to get models?

Fortunately, I work with local burlesque diva Sarah "Sparkly Devil" Klein, who eagerly volunteered to be our first model and is already scheming to recruit her fellow dancers to help us out.

My wife has been a "straight" artist's model for over 20 years, so she's been helpful with suggestions and payment guidelines and such, too. I've put my foot in my mouth a couple times describing Dr. Sketchy around my wife. "Y'know, it's like a life drawing class, but with *interesting* models! Er, uh, I mean...!!" (Sorry, honey!)"

Have you encountered any local resistance?

Well, not yet! We're probably still a little under-the-radar, so we'll see. One Hatch member is a local art school instructor and said some fellow instructors we're a bit put off by the "anti-art school" line on the flyers.

Was it easy or difficult to talk a venue into letting you put on some debauched life drawing?

Easy to talk them into it, harder to straighten out the details. Hopefully that'll get easier in the future.

How's the session going? Do you have any crazy stories?

Sarah is very proud of our having to eject a drunk creepy guy on our very first session. He went quietly. Other than that, our first session went amazingly well, everyone had a really great time, I'd say. At one point I looked out at the group, all flopped on sofas and chairs and the floor, laughing and chatting and working away at their art, and had a weird flashback to the Catholic youth group retreats I attended in high school. It was *that* cozy (of course, instead of a youth counselor and John Denver songs, we had a burlesque dancer and Tom Jones).

One of our contests was a "round robin" 20-minute pose, where everyone worked for five minutes, then dropped their sketchbook, moved one place to the left, and worked for the next five minutes on the drawing in their neighbor's book. The result was several four-artist collaborations that we all went around signing afterwards. The drawings were surprisingly good and a lot of fun to do!

DR. SKETCHY'S PHILADELPHIA

http://www.trinityartgallery.com/events_sketchys.php

Spunky Kiki Berlin of Dr. Sketchy's Philadelphia.

Genevive Zacconi

Gallery owner, artist, and mistress
of Dr. Sketchy's Philadelphia

Tell me a bit about the art scene in your city? Is it crazy? Decadent? Nonexistent? And what part do you think Dr. Sketchy's plays in it?

Philadelphia has a great underground Burlesque culture, but the art scene in here can be a bit conservative. I've made it my personal mission to change this. There are a few galleries in the Philadelphia arts district helping push the proverbial envelope; but I must say, (and I might be biased) that my gallery, Trinity, is pioneering the peddling of the most finely rendered smut . . . um . . . I mean "erotic art," helping to change this conservative, outdated outlook. Dr. Sketchy's is playing a vital part in this crusade.

What made you interested in sucking it up and producing your own Dr. Sketchys? Besides me badgering you, that is.

Shameless self-promotion. Juvenile rebelliousness. A love for art. A passion for uninhibited expression. My being a huge fan of the amazing Miss Molly Crabapple.

What do you do in real life? Are you a professional artist, or just a devotee of drawing scantily clad girls?

I am a professional fine artist and gallery owner.

Has it been hard or easy to get models?

EASY! The Hellcat Girls Burlesque troop has been great, and volunteered to have each of their girls do at least one session. I, luckily, also keep a few beautiful boy-toys on hand at all times, who are accounting for the male-model quota.

Have you encountered any local resistance?

Surprisingly, no! All of the other galleries seem really enthused about us doing the event and the Philadelphia City Paper even did an article on it.

How's the session going? Do you have any crazy stories? Lying absolutely encouraged.

For the first Dr. Sketchy's at Trinity, we had our model, Kiki Berlin outside of the gallery in a sequined bikini, feathered headpiece, and heels posing for pictures. There was nearly a car accident on the street. Men began cheering from their cars. When I announced to them that for a small cover fee they could see Miss Berlin *without* the bikini, a group of gentlemen pulled over and parked with great haste. They joined the group, surprised at how little the cover charge was, but consequently had a hefty fine to pay because of their rushed, and very illegal parking job.

HOW TO START YOUR OWN DR. SKETCHY'S

*A*dmit it: we've sold you. You want in on this delirious world of ink and nudity. Dr. Sketchy's is your passport to coolness, your tag of talent, your alt-indie street cred, the rocket you will ride to your rapidly burgeoning fame. It will also get you totally laid.

If you approach it right.

If you do it wrong, you'll be as unloved as middle school.

So, hearken here, dear reader and listen to the age-old secrets passed down from the first Dr. Sketchy's that parted Roman mists like a tavern wench's thighs. This is how it's done.

GETTING STARTED

*L*ike seduction or climbing Mt. Everest, plotting your first Dr. Sketchy's session is best broken into steps.

The Rules

★ Email me first! Molly@mollycrabapple.com. I am a megalomaniac who enjoys seeing her ideas reach fruition, and I want to keep an eye on you.

★ Treat your models well. Ravishing, interesting models are the foundation on which good art classes are built. Show your models respect. Pay them a good wage (at least 20 dollars an hour in big cities, a bit less in smaller ones). Encourage the artists to tip. Bring pillows and space heaters. Remember, models are the Dr. Sketchy stars. If you treat your models badly, the ghost of Kiki de Montparnasse will come back to life and beat you to death with a violin.

★ Don't hit on models, creep out artists, or act like a jerk. Don't be the heavy breather who smells like cat pee hovering over the girls. They never get laid.

★ Make a webpage, even a MySpace page. Exchange links with me. Distinguish yourself from our session by calling yourself Dr Sketchy's - Atlanta, or Dr. Sketchy's - Timbuktoo. The internet is our generation's Gutenberg. Without a site, you don't exist.

★ If you ever get into the press, pretty please mention us.

How to Do It

 Step One: The Venue

You want a place with a bit of seating, preferably one that serves coffee and booze. Many cafes and bars are slow during the day on weekends, and would be happy to have the extra people buying drinks. If you can't get a café or bar, try galleries, bookstores, or even a friend's big living room.

 Step Two: The Model

I prefer models with interesting careers. Burlesque girls, mimes, roller derby girls, human statues, vaudeville jugglers, bodybuilders, costume designers, and sideshow freaks are all great choices. Dancers of any genre make fantastic models. Let the model know she can go wild with her costume.

 Step Three: Find Sponsors for Your Contests

Dr. Sketchy's is all about cool contests. Whether the contest is "best left handed" drawing or "best incorporation of a squirrel," artists compete to win fabulous prizes.

To get free booty for your sketch class, approach local art stores, new restaurants, or your friend's dildo cozy business. Let them know that in exchange for a small donation they can get free banner advertising on your site, their logo on your flyer, and be mentioned frequently and annoyingly during the session.

Can't find sponsors? Make or buy stuff yourself, free passes to a new session are a great prize. And remember, everyone loves competing for a shot of liquor.

⭐ Step Four: The Budget

Figure out how much you're spending on models, prizes and promotion. Divide that by how many people you think will come. That's your door price. Try not to go over 10 bucks though, lest you cut into your attendance.

⭐ Step Five: Make Fliers

Put them up on art school campuses, bookstores, coffee shops, and anywhere else potential sketchers might hang out. Saturation postering yields surprisingly large results.

⭐ Step Six: Planning!

Typically, a life model poses for three hours, twenty minutes at a time, with five minute breaks in between and a twenty minute break in the middle. The NYC Dr. Sketchy's schedule is:

Length of Pose ⭐	Number of Pose
1 minute	10
2 minutes	5
5 minute break	
5 minutes	4
10 minutes	2
5 minute break	
20 minutes	1
20 minute break	
20 minutes	3 with 5 minute breaks in between

☆ ☆

During the breaks, we announce contests and give prizes. Helper Monkeys may amuse and delight with improtu go-going.

⭐ **Step Seven:** Draw, Dammit!

Essential Sketchy Supplies

⭐ Pillows, blankets or yoga mats for the model.

⭐ Clip lighting (available at Home Depot or a any large hardware store) with bright light bulbs. Place strategically so the room isn't pitch dark.

⭐ Cool nonsense to give away as prizes.

⭐ Change (dollar bills, fives and tens).

⭐ A box or jug in which to stick the model's tips.

⭐ Also nice but nonessential are cheap sketchpads and pens for the curious. More than a few people will drop in without drawing materials. You can sell these too for a tidy profit.

Wooing a Venue

*T*he thought of talking to the management of a place may scare you more than talking your girlfriend into anal. But fear not, would-be Sketchy disciple. Venues need you just as much as you need them. Here's how to get space for your nefarious deeds.

⭐ Scope out your neighborhood. Whether you live in Virginia or Paris, there are undoubtedly spaces that host events. It could be a bar, coffeeshop, club or even spacious bookstore. So make a list of all the places around that might be interested in having a life drawing class.

★ Get to know your few favorite venues. Stop by frequently. Buy drinks or coffee. If possible, chat with the owner.

★ Prepare your strategy. Venues need events to keep people coming, but they don't want to loan their space out to a dud. So you'll need to prove that you can get people out and buying drinks. Figure out the venue's slow times (often during the day for a bar). Tell them how you'll promote the dickens out of the event, perhaps comparing it to similar but not directly-competitive events that have captured the love of your city. Trot out any event-planning credentials. Present it as a win-win situation, wherein they get a new crowd while you get hot Sketchy action. Here's where a great webpage and a professional demeanor might help.

★ Email the owner. If this isn't possible, call up the venue and ask if there's a slow time you can drop by where the owner will be there. Give them a case as to why their venue will benefit, as well as several ways to contact you. Let them know that Dr. Sketchy's is already internationally successful, and that you'd essentially be opening a franchise—but without the ugly hats and polyester.

★ Bitter failure? Try try again.

★ To keep up good venue relations, clean up, thank profusely, and draw a crowd.

Wooing a Sponsor

If you've summoned up the courage to find a venue, you still might be stymied by sponsors. After all, why should anyone give you free stuff? If it were so easy, wouldn't everyone do it? Wouldn't you already be neck-deep in shotguns, hookers and blow?

The first thing you need is an idea of what you have to offer. You can give the companies a banner ad on top of your website, their logo on your poster, and a sloppy verbal blowjob when you're on the model stand.

It comes down to two things to offer. For big, established companies, you've got street cred. For cool indie businesses, you've got cheap advertisement.

Second, find the sort of companies that might give you their booty. Start small—the new retro diner that opened up, a friend's craft business. Post on web communities for small businesses and crafters, giving them a clear analysis of why it's super-duper awesome to sponsor Dr. Sketchy's. Try for businesses where there's a natural tie-in (art supply stores), but don't be afraid to ask for burlesque show passes or pornographic rug hooking kits either.

Once you've done a few sessions, sponsors are easier to come by. Revise your list of benefits to include how many people visit your website, subscribe to your mailing list and come to each session. Include all your media appearances from The New York Times to the Podunk Tribune.

When going after big companies, stress your grass roots appeal, media mentions and flat out coolness. If you shop with them, say so.

And remember, keep politely asking. It's not thievery. I"s an essential principle of marketing.

The Care and Feeding of Models

Ah, now for the part you're really interested in. How to get nubile girls to take off their clothes. Well, Lothario, I'm here to dash your hopes. I worked as a life model throughout college, and we're wise to your game. If your intentions are dishonorable, not only will you get no tail—but no models either.

Remember, modeling is a job. Most of the time, if anyone's uncomfortable with nudity, it's the person doing the hiring. The model just wants to turn a buck. Above all, don't act like you're tricking the model into something.

I founded Dr. Sketchy's to create the modeling experience I always wanted. I set my wages as high as any other place in New York and always encourage artists to tip. Between these two things, my model makes over $100 in three hours (more than any other place in NYC) and I have girls foxy-boxing to pose for me.

Remember Dr. Sketchy's models are performers as well as anatomical studies. So ask people in your local performing community. Burlesque and roller derby babes are my favorite, but this depends on what's available where you live. Since they are performers, treat them as such. Compliment them. Tell the audience how simply wonderful the models are and where they can be seen next. Put their names and pictures on everything. Encourage the artists to applaud after good poses. Treat them like stars.

But, you cry, "I live in a one Starbucks town, with no fierce and sultry performers!" Well, try posting notices at art schools, local colleges, and bookshops. Stress that the girls won't be naked, that the setting is public, and that there will be other girls there. Remember that modeling is hard labor. I blew out my left wrist posing. Because of this, treat your model well! Bring her pillows. Make sure the temperature is right. And never, ever try to make her hold a pose longer than agreed upon. This is why I can't bend my left wrist back.

With good pay, good treatment and good promotion, you'll find many, many people who will want to pose for your Dr. Sketchy's.

How to Get People to Show Up

𝓡emember, your audience has a glut of choices. Dr. Sketchy's competes with television, video games, strip bars, and natural inertia. . . . So promoting your event should be the most titanic, most gargantuan of your efforts. Here's a plan of attack.

 Use the Internet

There are many, many websites covering your area. Post to all of them. See bloggers who write about art? Email them, telling them about your fascinating event and asking them if they'd blog about it in exchange for a free seat. Ask your friends with websites to post copious infomation.

★ Listings

Notice those rags cluttering up your local coffee shop? Those rags exist to highlight you. Find the listings address, generally listings@bigimportantmagazine.com. Write up a two sentence description of your event, and include time, date, venue, address, webite and price. Send it along to the listings address, three weeks or so before they go to print. It might take a while, but eventually, they will list you. Both Daily Candy and Time Out ignored Dr. Sketchy's for months before giving in to the inky juggernaut.

★ Flyers

Make flyers and postcards. You can get 500 postcards printed up fairly easily by googling postcards and finding the best deal. Put them everywhere—but particularly where pretentious Art Monkeys gather. Coffee shops. Art stores. Add your flyers to the obnoxious visual clutter of your neighborhood. Carry around postcards and pass 'em out to people.

★ Mailing lists

Pass around a mailing list soliciting email addresses at every Dr. Sketchy's session. Set up an account with www.Constantcontact.com, put a signup box on your website, and send out mailings.

 Where to Stick Flyers

Art Stores   Colleges   Coffee Shops   The Entire District of your City
populated by "Heep-sters"   Inside art books at the book store
Scattered liberally at more staid art classes   Computer stores
Subway station exits   In the garter of Lady Blows-Alot
The events of your bitter rival

$\mathscr{G}$ot a rock star fantasy? So do we. Think of how much better you'd feel if you could spend a few brief moments cheered by drunken artists, your prize drawing held up, and your head swelled with cheap, transient fame?

Dr. Sketchy's contests raise the excitement and give people the love they never had as children. Although you might be a bit baffled as what to do, fear not dear reader. Here's an assortment of contest ideas. Adapt as needed.

Handicap contests

☆ Best drawing of figure in motion. Could your model go for go-go? Fan Dancing? Jerking about in a furious mumba wumba? Don't let this one go on too long though, lest the lady collapse.

☆ Best drawing done in under one minute

☆ Best drawing with off hand.

☆ Best drawing done in a 2" x 2" area

Embellishment contests

☆ Best incorporation of a woodland creature into the drawing

☆ Best rendering of the model as a mythical figure or fanciful beast

☆ Best placement of the model in an invented setting

☆ Best drawing of the model in an invented costume

☆ Best incorporation of a celebrity into the drawing

☆ Have each Art Monkey write a noun on a piece of paper, draw one at random and have the art monkeys incorporate that into the drawing

General contests

☆ Most lifelike

☆ Model's favorite

☆ Utterly Strangest

But how to judge? At the NYC Dr. Sketchy's we use applause, which is about as fair as a Soviet election. Try voting, obvious favoritism, or just leave it up to the model.

When the Model Doesn't Show
A Cautionary Tale
by Molly Crabapple

Once, I booked a famous burlesque dancer, but due to scheduling snafus, the lady didn't show. There I was, with ravenous artists and a television crew from HD.net. Luckily I lived three blocks from the Lucky Cat. I ran home, changed into something glittery and slutty, and modeled for the class myself.

Can't do that? Then harken to my lesson. Confirm two days in advance, with ALL the info in the email. Get the model's cellphone number. I had Leavitt pose in my place while I ran to polish off my sequined bikini. You never know your friend's lack of shame will come in handy.

ADVICE FROM SKETCH WORLD

Melanie Knight, Dr. Sketchy's Melbourne:

I highly recommend all aspiring sketchistas to have a love of drawing and a love of trying to make the time spent drawing as fabulous and fun as possible—what's a sketch class without feathers I say! Most of all get out there and support your local art scene and hopefully it will support you.

Jason Levesque, Dr. Sketchy's Norfolk:

Realize that Dr Sketchy's is going to take time. It takes a lot of flyering and "events posting" to grow the group. Ultimately it will be worth it. It's a wonderful feeling to see people pick up their sketchbook and pencil after years of not drawing. College art professors love the idea of extracurricular art groups, talk to them and ask them to post flyers. Also getting some press through your local paper will help tremendously. Good luck!

Rachael Bess, Dr. Sketchy's Phoenix:

I think a lot of people are nervous about coming out for the first time because they're afraid about not being skilled enough, but remember that everyone in the room started somewhere, and no one really cares if you drew the legs a little short or whatever. In my opinion, there's nothing that teaches drawing any better than the human figure so why not learn in a titillating environment! Also, always be respectful of the model, if you like what they do, tip them, or treat them to a Choco Taco!

Genevive Zacconi, Dr. Sketchy's Philadelphia:

Have liquor available at the event and encourage heavy drinking amongst the patrons . . . the drawings are way more interesting with intoxicated attendees.

Sean Bieri Dr. Sketchy's Detriot:

Well, I know that next time I'll have a sign-in sheet to collect email addresses, and bring a mix CD in case the model doesn't have one. Bring clamp lights and spare bulbs too, in case the lighting is too dim, as it often is in bars. Also, try the collaborative drawing thing, that was a blast!

A Super-Fun Dr. Sketchy's Colouring Book Page!
Little Brooklyn: Burlesque Comic and Dr. Sketchy Model

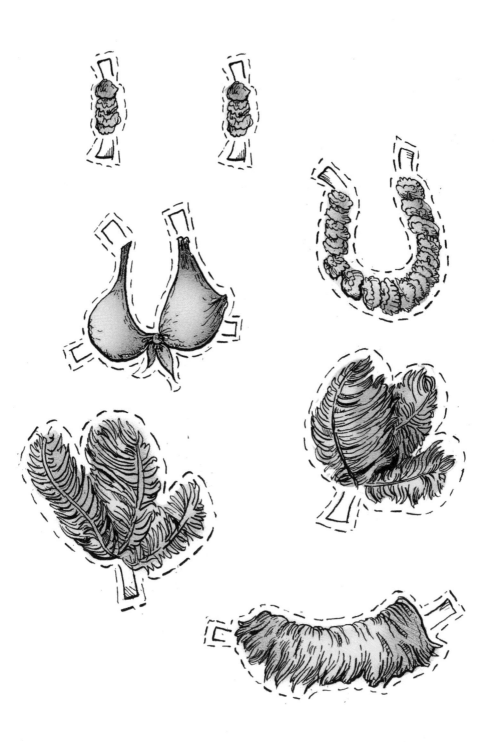

Cut out these paper dolls of Miss Allison and Darlinda Just Darlinda, fix with screws, and pose to your heart's content.

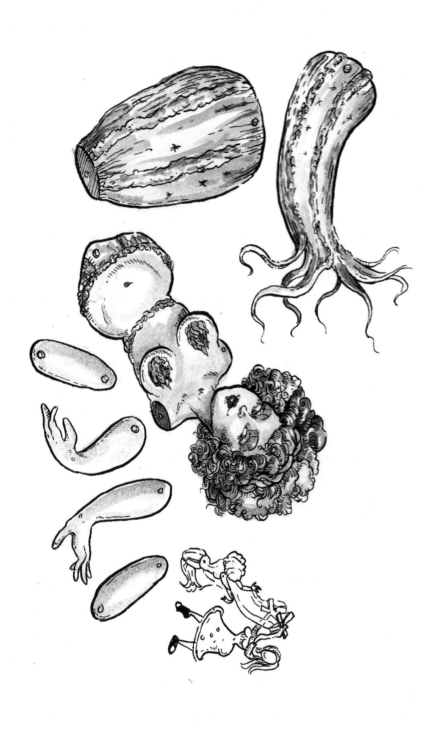

Miss Allision shakes her fans at Dr. Sketchy's NYC,
photographed by Dr. Simon

GIVE SOME HEAD

This poor model has gone and lost her head! Correct this freakish
drawing by giving her a new head. Send completed drawings to
drsketchy@gmail.com to win a fabulous prize! (or not)

Burlesque surrealist, Darlinda Just Darlinda at Dr. Sketchy's NYC,
photographed by Ryan Roman

Dr Sketchy's NYC: Lady J and Art Monkey Steve Walker,
photographed by Ryan Roman

Lady J, photographed by Ryan Roman

John Leavitt, photographed by Ryan Roman

Drawing of the lovely
Miss Allison from Art
Monkey and comic book
artist, Steve Walker

THE GAME OF DR. SKETCHY'S!

Live of the life of an artist without the tuition bills, poverty, and uncomfortable burning sensations! The Game of Dr. Sketchy's takes you from Podunk, U.S.A to fame and fortune, if you can manage to avoid poverty, jail, and death. For 2-4 players and a 6-sided die.

STATIONS

These circles are the phases in your young artist's life. If you pass one on a roll, you can choose to stop there instead of continuing your turn. In order to escape a station, you either have to roll an escape number or perform a degrading action to the delight of your friends.

Art School - Roll evens to escape or draw a portrait of the person next to you in under a minute.

Clubland - Roll odds to escape or perform a sexy mumba-wumba dance.

The Café - Roll odds to escape or expound at length about a topic you knowing about for a full 2 minutes.

The Office - The only no escape station. Stare blankly into space for 5 minutes. before moving on.

The Garret - Roll evens to escape or share a horrible apartment story.

The Clinic - Roll evens to escape or share an overdose-embarrassingly drunk story.

The Gallery - Roll evens to escape or hold up the picture you drew in the Studio to be harshly judged by the other players.

The Spotlight - Roll odds to escape or get another player to ask you an interview question.

The Studio - Roll odds or draw a picture to escape.

The Penthouse - Roll evens to escape or tear apart another player's fashion sense in a faux british accent.

HOLLYWOOD

Local Hero! Roll even to go to Cafe, Odd! to return Home

Bright Lights, Big City

Mom thinks you're cool. Move to Art School

Hey man, you wanna get high? Lose a turn, move ahead one space

Panic Attack! Return home, weeping

Rent Control Move ahead Three?

Horrifying Roomate Skip a Turn

Steal Paint Move ahead one

Bong hit?

Start a Band! Lose a turn

Buried in Slush Pile next three moves are one space

Blowjob in bathroom Everyone moves ahead four spaces?

Experiment with sexuality. Choose another player to share 5 spaces with, you speed.

Really Cheap Beer

Mother's Little Helper

Daddy's Money Runs out. Choose Debt or Office

Ironic Hair Wipe ahead two spaces

BOOZE?

FAIR TRADE

Trust fund kicks in Go to Clubland or get a free turn

Voodoo Doll. Move any player back one space

Drunk and Disorderly Lose a turn

Booze?

Hangover?

Booze?

The Porn Industry

Get into Comics Loose a turn geekhead

Condom Broke. Roll an even number to escape Baby

Bong Hit?

Botched Suicide Return home for observation

Coffee? Jitter too spaces ahead

Fancy Dinner! Skip a turn

Not Pretty anymore. Back to Art School.

Trip around the world Lose 2 turns

Doggy

It hurts to pee, go to Clinic

Eating Disorder! Go to Hollywood

Art Porn Go to Spotlight

Retail Porn miss a turn

WAWAWA BABY!

Student Loans Go to Debt

Facial Tattoo To to Garret

Bong Hit?

Pink slip Go back to garret to get a free roll

Graduate Study Back to Art School

Uberton Slut?

$HORTCUTS

What would life be without unfair advantages? These shortcuts can only be used if you land on or choose to stop at a Station. You must declare your intent to use the shortcut "before" rolling. If you overshoot the shortcut by rolling more than the number spaces to the other end, you loose your turn and go nowhere.

#RISONS

An Artist's life is fraught with challenges and danger. Babies, Old Time Religion, Hollywood, Debt, they can all grind your carrer to a halt. Upon escaping a prison, you return to the square you where last at..

Hollywood and Debt - Roll a 1, 2, or 3 to escape.
Baby and Old Time Religion - Roll a 4, 5, or 6 to escape.

#NE #FF

Patronage, Tell All Memoir, Shoot Andy Warhol.

These three squares are like Shortcuts except they only have one square. You can only access them from a Station, but you can choose to use them no matter what you roll.

Suggestions For Game Pieces:

Pennies. Thimbles. Pieces from other games. Lint. Ornate silver figurines. Your own finger.

Remember, you don't have to move ahead. Sometimes a calculated step backward avoids risks up-ahead. Now have fun and play nice..

Can't get any nifty prizes for Contests? No trouble! Simply cut out this "Official Dr. Sketchy's Diploma," sign it, and present it to the winning Art Monkey. It's good for one free session and a lot more useful than most art degrees.

Dr. Sketchy's Anti-Art School

By the Authority Of A Hearing Mob Of Art Monkeys Art

And Upon The Recommendation of the Drunken Idiots

Who ran it

Has been awarded

One Free Session

Upon Presentation of this Document

Valid Only With Signature

_____
Dr. Sketchy's Operator

_____
Dr. Archibald Sketchy, Dean

Lady J and a lucky contest winner at Dr. Sketchy's NYC, photographed by Gary Winter

GOOD IDEAS

You've got models lined up, a kick-ass venue, and posters all over town. What else can you do to make the whole thing go down like champagne? The following tips will have you and your Monkeys swinging and cheering the whole night through.

The Stage

All of life may be a stage, but not all stages are created equal. The ideal venue has a raised platform large enough to lie down on. Putting the model on top of the bar may seem terribly bohemian, but it's more trashy than artsy, disrupts normal bar service and may have your models falling onto the Monkey's heads. Set out pillows and a chair for longer poses; your model's back will thank you.

If no stage can be found, use amateur theater cunning. A few heaps of blanket and pillows make an effective stand-in. Stairs will do a pinch; just make sure no one plans on using them anytime soon.

Seating

Typical life drawing classes are painfully low on chairs, leading to bruised bums, weak knees, and simmering resentment. Buck this trend with chairs, couches, cushions, or a decadent chaise-lounge. Bars and cafes may loathe giving up their prime derriere real-estate, so a few cushions from home will make your Monkeys happy.

When setting out chairs or cushions, be mindful of sight lines and clear bathroom routes. Fire regulations aside, no one wants to step over sketchpads and spilled drinks just to use the loo. If your venue has couches, consider selling reservations to avoid fights over who gets the overstuffed daybed. Same goes for tables.

Know Your Venue

Don't be a shadowy figure to your hosts. Get to know the owners and staff of your venue. Chat them up about slow hours, safety codes, and the particular local laws about alcohol being served near nipples. If you become a fixture (especially a profitable fixture), owners may let you use storage closets or extra stools. Nothing beats having your lights and pillows already at hand, saving time and your weary arms.

As it is with life, context is key. Is your venue an all-night booze-up or a comfy cafe? Gothy models and heavy makeup may be a hit at Club Despair, not so much the Pink Poodle Coffeshop. Knowing the tone and spirit of your venue will create that "synergy" thing businessmen like to talk about.

Mise En Scene

No one likes blank backgrounds. Use that aforementioned amateur theater cunning to create dramatic backdrops for your models. Compose the model and background as you would a painting. A comfy chair with a table gives it a living room atmosphere. Position them against the local artwork no doubt on display in the more artsy cafes and bars. A stained painter's drop cloth behind the model gives you Abstract Expressionist credibility. Mirrors help everyone and allow for more interesting compositions.

Goodies

*F*ree stuff is the best stuff and starving Art Monkeys like free food even more. A discount bag of pretzels keeps monkeys happy and thirsty and drink tickets for the models inspire return visits.

Don't be bound by age or good taste. Party favors unlock the toddler in all of us. Bubble guns, crayons, coloring books and noisemakers make any event festive. Besides, who doesn't want to see a room full of adults with paper hats and kazoos?

Poses

*O*ne minute, Two minute, Five minute, Ten . . . the format of life-drawing can be as formal as Japanese poetry and just as exciting. A frantic five minute go-go in lieu of a pose breaks up monotony and gives your model's joints some well-earned lubrication. Is your model a performer? If so, make use of her talents. A feat of juggling or contortionism adds vaudeville flair to your lineup. One of our models, Lady J, brought her band along for songs between sets. Try classic poses with new props. Michelangelo's "David" always looked like a golfer anyway. Use these acts sparingly however; this is a life drawing class, not a night at the Improv.

The Tip Jar

*N*ix the dollars tucked in the g-string, this ain't the Pussycat Lounge. Instead, have a tip jar front and center, reminding the Monkeys that good poses deserve good payment. Be creative with your jars. At the Lucky Cat our tip jar is just that, a plastic cat's head. One clever model used her parasol to collect hard-won bills.

Tunes and Tribulations

*E*ar-shattering death metal may be your preferred soundtrack at home, but not everyone appreciates Whitesnake. Strive for a volume above audible but below conversation killing. Soft doesn't mean boring however. Would Toulouse-Lautrec have drawn such vivacious dancers without the Can-

Can? The right music can add that extra layer that turns a drab modeling session into a veritable hootenanny.

Consider theme CDs for different models. Brassy New Orleans jazz for burlesque queens or rockabilly fever for Punk Rock Gods. For a few set play lists guaranteed to inspire, check out these Sketchy Mixes created by mix-master Leavitt.

Big Bad and Beautiful

This mix is bursting with classic cheekiness and dirty ditties. Perfect for your Burlesque classicists with fans, tassels, and 'tude.

1. Bumps & Grinds - Sonny Lester & His Orchestra
2. Bounce Your Boobies - Sophie Tucker
3. Flight of the Passing Fancy - Squirrel Nut Zippers
4. Meet Me In the Red Room - Isobel Griffiths
5. When You're Good to Momma - Queen Latifah
6. My Heart Belongs To Daddy - Marilyn Monroe And Cole Porter
7. When You've Got it, Flaunt It - The Producers, Original Cast Recording
8. You've Got to See Momma Every Night - Sophie Tucker
9. Apres Moi - Eartha Kitt
10. Milord - Edith Piaf
11. Cabaret - Liza Minnelli
12. I'll Build a Stairway to Paradise - Rufus Wainright
13. Whatever Lola Wants - Sarah Vaughn
14. Why Don't You Do Right? - Amy Irving
15. My Champagne Tastes - Eartha Kitt
16. Brazil - Carmen Miranda

Oi! Oi! Oh Boy!

A perfect collection of music for when your model is more Joan Jett than Gypsy Rose Lee.

1. She's So Modern - The Boomtown Rats
2. Ever Fallen In Love - The Buzzcocks
3. Girl U Want - Devo
4. Cherry Bomb - The Runaways
5. Words and Guitar - Sleater-Kinney
6. X Offender - Blondie
7. Gimmie My Radio - The Donnas
8. Beat City - The Raveonettes
9. Trash - New York Dolls
10. Ballroom Blitz - Sweet
11. Tear Me Down - Hedwig And the Angry Inch
12. S-E-X-X-Y - They Might Be Giants
13. Boys Keep Swinging - David Bowie
14. Roadrunner - The Modern Lovers
15. She's a Rainbow - The Rolling Stones
16. Sister Midnight - Iggy Pop

Mondo Bizzaro

Music for when your model decides to dress as an Anime Kitten Superhero from the future.

1. Electric Lady Land - Fantastic Plastic Machine
2. Pop Muzik - Ex-Girl
3. Ca Plane Pour Moi - Plastic Bertrand
4. Interplanet Janet - Man Or Astroman?
5. Prince Charming - Adam and The Ants
6. I, Monster - The Blue Wrath
7. I'm on E - Blondie
8. Dorisdaytheearthstoodstill - Future Bible Heroes
9. Life on Mars - David Bowie

10. Superstars Of Bollywood - Momus
11. Keys to Her Ferrari - Thomas Dolby
12. I Just Can't Get Enough - Depeche Mode
13. Gessekai Toshi - Shonen Knife
14. Tokyo FM - Pizzicato Five
15. The Ballad Of Lucy Jordan - Marianne Faithful
16. But You're So Beautiful - Future Bible Heroes

Hipper Than Thou

This mix blends classic and modern themes, guaranteed to have your
hipster Monkeys nodding their heads in approval.

1. Come Dancing - The Kinks
2. I'm Sorry That I Love You - The Magnetic Fields
3. Generation Sex - Divine Comedy
4. I Know What Boys Like - The Waitresses
5. Lips Like Sugar - Echo and the Bunnyman
6. Going Underground - The Jam
7. Mucha Muchacha - Esquivel
8. Wedding Samba - Carmen Miranda
9. I Want You But I Don't Need You - Momus
10. Ceremony - New Order
11. Denis - Blondie
12. Oh Boy! - Buddy Holly
13. Land Of A Thousand Dances - Wilson Pickett
14. Coin Operated Boy - The Dresden Dolls
15. Pretty In Pink - The Psychedelic Furs
16. Windmills Of Your Mind - Dusty Springfield

Hand Exercises

As any teenage boy can tell you, repetitive motions produce painful hands and aching wrists. Save money on carpal tunnel treatments with a few simple exercises. Perform the following right before drawing and once again for every twenty min of continuous drawing or whenever you start to feel stiff.

* Stretch your fingers out as far as they will go. Hold for five seconds, and then release. Repeat three times.

* Make a fist. Rotate your wrist from side to side a few times.

* With your arm at your side, bend your wrist fully up. Hold for ten seconds, and then bend it back towards you. Hold for five seconds.

* Let your wrist go floppy, wave it around a bit like a delicate lady shooing away a fly. Trust me, this one works.

* Hold your palm up as if you're singing "Stop! In the Name of Love." Touch your fingers to your palm five times. Make a fist and hold it for five seconds. Repeat three times.

* Finally, just relax your hand. Go grab a drink, let it lay limp on the table. You may look like a dork, but you won't end up wearing an even dorkier wrist brace.

Invisible Ink

Fulfill your lifelong dream of being a super-secret spy with invisible ink contests. Hand out quills and small cups of lemon juice. Have your monkeys draw the model (one-five minute pose only, please, no one wants to stare at a blank page for twenty minutes) and then place the invisible drawings on a radiator or near a 100 watt bulb. Ironing the paper works too, just make sure to not to singe the paper. For those ill-inclined or ill-prepared to heat up paper, borrow a stoner friend's black light and hand out Invisible U.V. ink pens. They are usually sold as Security Marker Pens and run about $2-5 each. Try a "Best Incorporation of an Occult Message" contest, combining traditional and invisible inks. Winner gets to keep the pen.

> If people think this is "stupid," remind them it's blind contour drawing.

Ex Libris

𝒯he following books should be a part of any Art Monkey's collection.

Jack Hamm, <u>Drawing the Head and Figure</u>. A must-have cheat-sheet for drawing people and faces, provided you want them to look like a 40's detective comic.

Betty Edwards, <u>Drawing on the Right Side of the Brain</u>. Proof that anyone can learn to draw with simple, easy to follow exercises. Great for beginners or someone looking to brush up their hand-eye skills. Art school meets neuroscience!

George Bridgeman, <u>Constructive Anatomy</u>. Big, serious reference book for drawing every muscle, every joint, and every ligament.

John Cody, <u>Visualizing Muscles</u>. Designed for medical students but perfect for artists, it has an innovative way of studying muscles. The model in the photos has the major muscle groups painted onto his rippling form.

Arthur L. Guptill, <u>Rendering in Pen and Ink</u>. Still looking for Carpal Tunnel? Molly swears by this 20's reference guide to stippling your way to success.

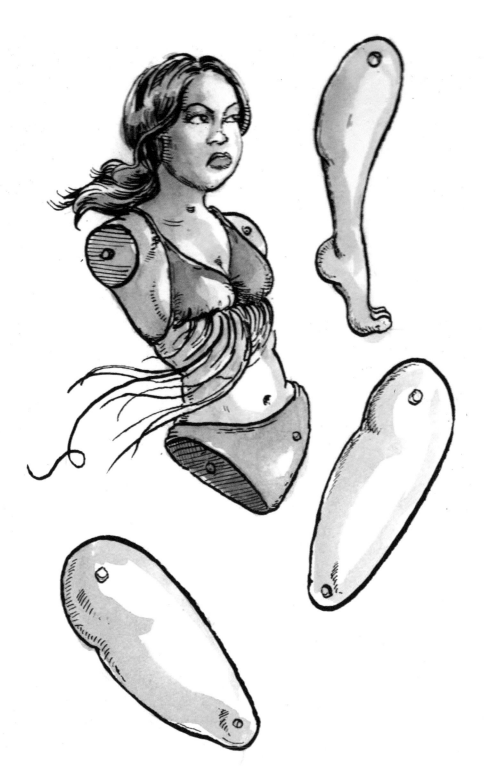

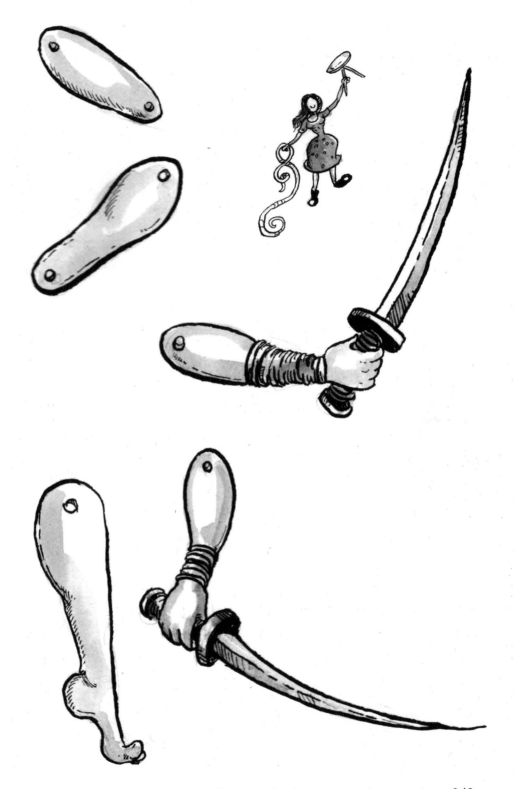

Daeta and Syd demonstrate the cruel fate to all art monkeys who don't tip the models. Let this be a lesson to you. Photo by Gary Winter.

BAD IDEAS

$\mathcal{U}$nlike the previous chapter, nothing in here is helpful. They are insane, chaotic, dangerous, and possibly illegal, possibly fun, but not helpful. Perform at your own risk.

The Espresso Game

$\mathcal{A}$ game with no winners, the espresso game is a drawing contest between two audience members. The model poses for five two minute poses. After each pose, the model chooses a winner. The winner receives a shot of espresso, no sugar, no lemon. At the end of five poses, the one with the most empty espresso cups is declared the "winner." The winner receives gets applause, a fabulous prize, and a ride to the nearest hospital.

Played with shots of alcohol, this game goes from Bad Idea to Spectacularly Bad Idea. Use caution, as this is a great way to lose a liquor license and/or cause Art Monkeys to drown in their own vomit.

Full Contact Modeling

$\mathcal{G}$ot two models? Time for a fight! A series of dramatic group poses make for more exciting tableaus. Drag Helper Monkeys onto the stage and put them in compromising positions. Models Ian and Gavin lit up the Dr. Sketchy stage with a whip, a hoop, and a lion tamer's outfit. Use discretion however, you don't want to go to the clink for running an unlicensed Foxy-Boxing tournament.

𝒮omewhere around the second Dr. Sketchy's, the blatantly alcoholic John Leavitt decided that what we needed was more booze. Now, one of the most beloved Dr. Sketchy's contests is the shot prize. Around the middle of the session, we throw a contest where the prize is a double shot of alcohol. But not just any alky. Leavitt handpicks the most ferocious and vile blends, which the "winner" then downs in one gulp.

Thus the modern world is amused.

Here are a few drink recipes, including one from amateur artist Aleister Crowley. When in doubt, use vodka. Lots of vodka.

French Whore

Taste isn't nearly as bad as the name. Provides endless opportunity for bad jokes. Do you know what's in a French whore?

2 parts Vodka

1 part Chambord

Sweet & Sour mix

Serve in Shotglass

Killer Kamikaze

Surprisingly pleasant, though menacing to say. Whip out this fruit concoction when a "girl" wins your contest. Leavitt warns it may cause unexplained vomiting.

1 part Vodka

1 part Triple Sec

1 part Lime Juice

Serve in Shotglass

Chartreuse

Ah, the goth drink. Chartreuse is as greasy and unpleasant as a hippy herbal store.

Serve straight to annoying artists who insist on "proper lighting."

Moscow Mule

Because we all want to deepthroat something Russian.

2 parts (6 cl) Vodka

1 part (24 cl) Ginger Beer

The Ink Blotto

Mom was right; never ingest anything black or bigger than your head. Serve in a chilled martini glass with a cherry. Just don't mistake it for your ink well.

1 part Blavod Black Vodka

half a part of Blackberry liqueur

1 part Dark Rum

The 20 Minute Pose

Long pose? Can't concentrate? This drink will keep you up and peppy, or make it so you no longer care about accurate rendering. Either way, it's a smash hit. Serve over ice in a coffee cup.

1 part Café Boheme, or other coffee liquor

A shot of Espresso

1 part Amaretto

Garnish with Lemon

Watercolor Pastiche

A drink that's fun to look at but decidedly less fun to drink. Blue Curacao is both distasteful and has a reputation for making your whole digestive tract colorful.

1 part Blue Curaco

1 part Cranberry Juice

1 part Cream

The Kubla Kahn   2

A recipe from that old reprobate
Crowley—amateur artist,
mountain climber and prophet
of the new millennium. Toxic
and illegal, we recommend
serving this one in a skull-
preferably not a plastic one.

Nicked from Crowley's Diary of a
Drug Fiend. Make up your own
Proportions.

Gin

Calvados

Creme de Menthe

Laudanum

Mix thoroughly, start beneath your
eyebrows, and declare yourself
Ipsissimus. We did.

A Super-Fun Dr. Sketchy's Colouring Book Page! 150

ART MONKEYS

$\mathscr{R}$emember, those heaving hordes of delinquents are actually people! Almost. They're Art Monkeys, the howling peanut gallery upon which Dr. Sketchy's success rests. Happy Art Monkeys will catapult you to fame and riches. Angry Art Monkeys will tear you from limb to limb and use your teeth for kitschy earrings.

A Rough Guide To Art Monkeys
Cartoons by J. Leavitt

The Floater

Moves from table to table, from seat to seat, chatting up people and checking out drawings. Excess coffee has made him jittery and given him a strong desire to stand around. Never seems to do any drawing.

The Crouching
Masturbator

This man smells like pee. Old pee.
He sits in the corner drawing the
same line over and over and giving
double-C creepy looks to the models.
Eliminate with extreme prejudice.

The Artiste

Actual artists who have no idea
how they got here. Comes early,
takes over tables with elaborate
supplies and arcane materials.
Serious expression. Never enters
contests despite (or because of) being
a shoo-in.

The Retired Art Teacher

Brings own folding chair. Scowls heavily. Makes desparaging comments about your lighting and the model's costume. Your online booking system confuses and enrages them. If they bother you, steal their pills.

The Party Girls

They're here for a good time and nothing will stop them. Their mouths get about as much exercise as their hands while they take unfair advantage of the cafe's cheap beer policy.

The Computer Guy

Yes, he brings a computer! Always a laptop, always with a wacom tablet, always a Mac, and always a high-end machine. You have to admire their tenacity to lug a heavy machine to sketch with, but all these computer fetishes point to a high paying job a sizable paycheck. Secretly hate them.

The Feeler

She's "getting in touch with her creativity" and exploring "feminine moon power." Wears batik. Quiet until you get a few drinks into her. Then it's all dancing around the fire and shouting to the Coyote Spirit.

The Drunk Doodler

He's drawing, kinda. The Drunk Doodler has a small pen and pad at the bar and is doing "free-style" drawing. After all, it's not drinking alone in a bar at 3pm if you're making art in the process!

The Regulars

Your old stalwarts. They've been coming since the first session and have generated enough good karma to become Helper Monkeys. You trust your regulars with props, the models, and the music. Still, they never win contests, because they already own all the merch.

The Animators

Very, very diligent. Animation students are some of the most compulsively hard working artists on the planet and it shows. Pages of drawings, a steely gaze, and a nasty habit of winning contests using word bubbles and superheroes.

The Tattoo Artist

Your walking, talking street-cred. Carries her portfolio on her skin. Considered twenty minutes to be "too short" to create anything worthwhile.

$\mathcal{R}$egular Art Monkeys may be employed to help out, thus vaulting them to the level of Helper Monkey. Helper Monkeys are your extra eyes and hands, setting out chairs, watching the door, and enduring public shame via forced Go-Go. Helper Monkeys are also invaluable for promotion, sending out mailing lists, posting to message boards, or filling blogs with hot Dr. Sketchy action. Repay their ceaseless devotion with free admission and drinks.

THE DR. SKETCHY CODE

The following letter was found at the scene of a ghastly crime at the Metropolitan Museum of Art in New York City. The curator was found in the Egyptian wing, mummified and placed in a Middle Kingdom tomb previously inhabited by Rhamses The Really Excellent. It was four days before anyone noticed the switch. The letter itself was stuffed inside the former curator's desiccated mouth. Authorities are asking for any help in untangling the seemingly nonsense phases.

Scandal! HotShot TricKery!

— — . — — — — — — — ' — —

— — — — — - — — — —

— — — — — —

Man Reworks Riddees!

— — — — — — — —

— — — — — . — — — — —

Hint: The first letter of both phrases is "D".

Joey Hardcore of the Gotham Girls Roller Derby chats with
Molly Crabapple, photographed by Gary Winter

A Super-Fun Dr. Sketchy's Colouring Book Page!

Ian And Gavin: Dancers and the very first Dr. Sketchy male models

Draw the Dr. Sketchy Way!

1.

First, draw an oval. That should be easy enough. It all starts with a circle. All creation begins with a circle; eggs, wombs, polyps, all circles.

2.

Now you draw another oval. That shouldn't be too hard. You can't have just one nowadays. Medical science has seen to that, the bastards.

3.

Draw other circles for nipples. Yea that's right, oh yeah, daddy likes his nipples. Draw um big and juicy. Oh baby.

4.

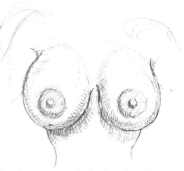

Use the science of "shading", or drawing lots of little lines, to really make those gorgeous melons pop. Some on the right, some on the left. Looking good. Looking very good. I may need another drink Ackmed! The wine!

5.

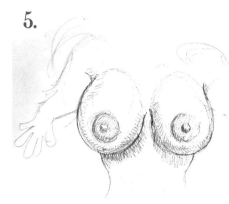

Where was I? Oh yes, the other bits. Um, well I guess girls need arms and stuff. Just throw one on there, just to the left of those luscious ripe snack trays over there. You know the deal, five fingers and a thumb.

6.

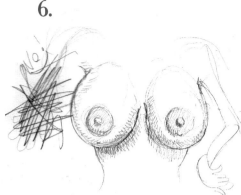

No! That's not right. Arms are longer! Girl arms anyway. Now cross that off and do the other one. Don't worry about details, art is about the big picture! The big, round, pert picture.

7.

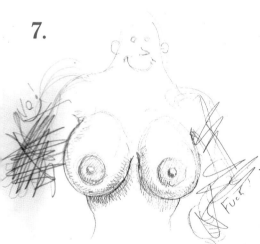

Girls also have heads and shoulders and other parts. Just put those to kinda on top of those ovals you drew before. My God. It's like they follow you around the room. Top off my drink boy!

8.

No that doesn't work at all! Just scrape the whole thing. Leave the breasts as they are. Those perfect, bounding breasts. They're .. looking at me. Questioning. Probing. It's like they see into my very Soul! Ackmed! Take away the art desk! Bring me the servant boy, a flagon of sparkling white wine and a gallon of Cocoa Butter. Daddy Sketchy needs to relax.

CONCLUSION

Alas, it is time for us to leave you, dear Reader. The book has run its course. And if it has done its job, you're now spent and prone. Creating Dr. Sketchy's has transformed our lives. We get to throw a party every other Saturday and get paid to do so. A silly fantasy of bohemian excess has been turned into shimmying reality after hard work, luck, and the undeniable power of beautiful girls. We couldn't be more proud.

To the thirteen-year old who has stolen this book, let me say something to you. You can do it! Cool things don't have to happen to other people! Take charge of your one-horse town, make something fun, amazing, witty, and hopefully profitable. It just takes a good idea and lots of effort. Shine on you crazy diamond.

- Molly Crabapple and John Leavitt
2006, NYC

AWESOME WEBSITES

www.drsketchy.com

Gaze Upon Our Artists

Fred Harper
www.fredharper.com

Jason Levesque
www.stuntkid.com

Genevive Zacconi
www.genevive.com

Mike Schwartz
www.mimo.awardspace.com

Sean Bieri
www.themanwhojaped.blogspot.com

Rachel Bess
www.rachelbess.com

Oogle Our Models

Dottie Lux
www.dottielux.com

Joey Hardcore
www.gothamgirlsrollerderby.com

Little Brooklyn
www.brooklyngirl.com

Tangerine Jones
www.tangerinejones.com

Audra Gwarskitty
www.gwarskitty.com

Kiki Berlin
www.hellcatgirls.com

Dolores Daiquiri
www.hiballburlesque.com

Daeta
www.daeta.com

Amber Ray
www.amberray.net

Sparkly Devil
www.sparklydevil.com

Lolita Haze
www.lolitahaze.com

Darlinda Just Darlinda
www.darlindajustdarlinda.com

Molly Crabapple is an award-winning artist, writer and the founder of Dr. Sketchy's Anti-Art School.

Crabapple learned to draw in a Parisian bookstore. She later drew her way through Morocco and Kurdistan, and once into a Turkish jail. Back in New York, she got her first illustration job doing covers for SCREW Magazine. She now wields her drawing pen for The New York Times, Wall Street Journal, Playgirl, as well as jugglers, fire-eaters, and blogs that sell used panties.

Crabapple is equally known for her fine art. Her surreal, sexy Victoriana hangs in galleries across the countries, as well as at the Coney Island Museum and the Museum of American Illustration.

While her high-school novel is thankfully confined to oblivion, Crabapple writes smart-aleck essays for places like New York Press, Punk Planet, Coagula Arts Journal, and a monthly column for Art Calendar.

During college, Crabapple worked as an art model, appearing scantily-clad (if at all) on Nerve, Suicide Girls and Lowrider. Because of this, she makes lists like New York Post's "25 Sexiest New Yorkers." and Fleshbot's "Top Ten Hotties of 2005." She's danced burlesque and eaten fire in dive bars in New York, New Jersey and Boston, once opening for the Dresden Dolls. Yes, she gets strange e-mails.

In December 2005, Crabapple founded Dr. Sketchy's Anti-Art School with her friend A.V. Phibes. Disappointed by the dull life drawing classes she'd posed for, Crabapple founded Dr. Sketchy's on the principles of fair pay for models and boozy fun for all. Artists draw burlesque dancers, compete in contests, and win liquor and prizes. Dr. Sketchy's has scooped up copious media love from places like NBC, Time Out NY, and the Village Voice.

Crabapple enjoys drinking coffee, drawing mean pictures and planning how to conquer Russia in the winter.

Her work can be seen at www.mollycrabapple.com

Contrary to popular myth and folklore, John Leavitt did not emerge fully formed from a dimension of unspeakable horror just beyond our perception. He comes from New Jersey.

After dropping out of college in New York, John was struck with the insane idea of becoming a cartoonist. He has appeared in the *New Yorker*, *The Chronicle Review*, the *New York Press*, and other places too monstrous to name. He performs burlesque, stand-up, and the occasional go-go for discriminating gentlemen.

John Leavitt is 22, lives in New York City, and may or may not have a drinking problem.

His work can be seen at www.jleavitt.net

CONTRIBUTORS' BIOS

Cause we love you guys.

Artists

A.V. Phibes co-ran the first Dr. Sketchy's with Molly Crabapple. She's an award winning artist, fast-talking business-lady and girl about town.

Fred Harper is a former wrestling champ and former carny. Since then, he's found success in almost every aspect of the illustration business, though he gets paid the most to draw mean pictures of the very powerful. He did the key art for 2005 Ozzfest.

Steve Walker is a survivor of School Of Visual Arts and a former designer in the low cost t-shirt business. He spends most of his time drawing comics. Steve can be coerced into writing the odd biographical blurb, depending if the right sacrifice has been made by the high priests of mu. He likes his coffee black with four sugars. Not three. Four.

Raina Bajpai is a painter living and working in Bushwick, Brooklyn. Her most recent project was an evening as artist-in-residence at Woodhull Medical Center.

Photographers

Dr. Simon Ben-Avi is an enigma, wrapped in a riddle, wrapped in crunchy nugget filling.

Ryan Roman is best known as the cartoonist behind Li'l Racists. He posts adorable porn on LiveJournal and talks guys into posing naked.

Jo "Boobs" Weldon is an award-winning burlesque performer, producer, photographer, and teacher living in New York City for as long as she possibly can. She is also a sex workers' rights advocate and essayist. She is thrilled to have contributed to Molly's book because she thinks Molly is da bomb.

Gary Winter's work as a photographer has largely gone unpublished, unprinted and unseen. But his lack of social graces and a tragic (some say pathetic) inability to interact productively with the human race made him a natural choice to document the important work being done by Dr. Sketchy's. Details of Mr. Winter's life remain largely unknown, particularly so to Mr. Winter.

Dr. Sketchy's Principals

Jason Levesque, aka Stuntkid is a graphic designer, painter and digital artist. His work has appeared on everything from computer art magazine covers to ads for erotic latex. Yes, the drawing of him was from life.

Mike Schwartz paints and runs the Atalier Mimo in Randers, Denmark.

Melanie Knight is an artist and art aficionado who works for the Melbourne Symphony Orchestra.

Rachel Bess is a classical oil painter. She paints angels guts, dead things, and machines that slowly destroy drawings. Rachel has hair like Louise Brooks.

Sean Bieri is an underground cartoonist and art director for Detroit's Metro Times.

Genevive Zacconi is pop surrealist oil painter. She runs Trinity Gallery, one of the most cutting-edge art spaces to scandalize old-city Philadelphia. When she drinks enough, she occasionally shakes it on the go-go platform.